Education and Learning Informatics

Revolutionizing the Future of Education through Data and Technology

By Oluchi Ike

Preface:

In the digital age, education is undergoing a profound transformation driven by the integration of informatics and cutting-edge technologies. The traditional classroom is evolving into dynamic, data-driven environments that are personalized, adaptive, and more engaging than ever before. Informatics—the science of processing data for storage and retrieval—has become a cornerstone of modern educational technologies, impacting how we design, deliver, and assess learning experiences.

This book, Education and Learning Informatics, explores the vital role of informatics in shaping the future of education. From personalized learning systems to gamified virtual environments, and from online education platforms to data-driven assessments, we will delve into the innovations that are transforming learning into a more personalized, engaging, and effective process. Whether you are an educator, administrator, policy-maker, or student, this book will provide you with insights into how informatics is redefining education and how it can be harnessed to create better learning experiences for all.

I hope this book serves as a guide for navigating the intersection of informatics and education, and that it sparks conversations on how we can continue to improve learning systems in the years to come.

Table of Contents:

Chapter 4: Gamification in Education

- The Principles of Gamification

- Virtual Learning Environments and Their Educational Benefits

- How Gamification Enhances Student Engagement and Motivation

Chapter 5: Data Analytics in Educational Assessment

- Understanding Educational Data Analytics

- How Data-Driven Assessments Improve Learning Outcomes

- Real-Time Analytics and Feedback Systems

Chapter 6: Virtual Classrooms and Remote Learning Tools

- The Growth of Virtual Classrooms Post-COVID-19

- Best Practices for Implementing Virtual Learning

- The Future of Remote Education

Chapter 7: Adaptive Learning Systems and AI in Education

- The Role of Artificial Intelligence in Adaptive Learning

- AI-Powered Educational Tools and Resources

- How AI is Transforming the Learning Process

Chapter 8: The Role of Data Privacy and Ethics in Educational Informatics

- Data Privacy Concerns in Educational Technologies

- Ethical Considerations for Student Data

- Developing a Framework for Ethical Data Use in Education

Chapter 9: Challenges and Opportunities in Learning Informatics

- Barriers to Adoption of Educational Technologies
- Opportunities for Innovation in Learning Informatics
- The Future of Education in a Data-Driven World

Chapter 10: Conclusion

- The Long-Term Impact of Informatics on Education
- How to Prepare for Future Changes in Educational Technologies
- Final Thoughts on the Role of Informatics in Shaping the Future of Learning

---

This structure will guide readers through a comprehensive understanding of how informatics and technology are transforming modern education.

Chapter 1: Introduction to Learning Informatics

The Evolving Role of Technology in Education

The role of technology in education has shifted dramatically over the past few decades. What began as the use of computers in classrooms has evolved into fully digital learning environments where technology drives not just the way students access information, but how they engage with content, interact with educators, and collaborate with peers. Education technology (EdTech) is no longer a supplementary tool—it is central to the delivery of modern education.

From the early days of simple computer labs and educational software to today's sophisticated digital learning management systems, technology has expanded the accessibility, flexibility, and reach of education. The COVID-19 pandemic accelerated this shift, with schools, universities, and training programs worldwide adopting online learning methods out of necessity. Remote learning, virtual classrooms, and hybrid models became the norm, further embedding technology into the fabric of education.

This digital transformation has given rise to learning informatics, a field that focuses on the application of data and computational techniques to enhance educational processes.

As technology evolves, so too does the potential for more personalized and adaptive learning experiences. Students can now learn at their own pace, access a wealth of online resources, and engage with interactive tools that cater to their unique learning styles. Educators, on the other hand, benefit from data-driven insights that allow them to assess student performance more accurately and tailor instruction accordingly. The role of technology in education is not just about convenience or efficiency—it's about revolutionizing the way we teach and learn.

What is Learning Informatics?

Learning informatics is the interdisciplinary field at the intersection of education, data science, and information technology. It involves the collection, analysis, and application of educational data to enhance learning outcomes and improve the efficiency of educational systems. Learning informatics goes beyond simply digitizing educational materials; it leverages data to understand student behaviors, learning patterns, and academic performance, with the goal of creating more personalized and adaptive learning environments.

In practical terms, learning informatics encompasses the use of algorithms, data analytics, artificial intelligence (AI), and machine learning to support educational decision-making and curriculum design. By analyzing vast amounts of data generated by students—ranging from quiz scores to time spent on specific topics—learning informatics provides insights that educators can use to optimize instruction. Additionally, it allows for the creation of systems that adapt to individual learners, offering tailored recommendations and interventions.

The ultimate aim of learning informatics is to create a dynamic feedback loop where data informs teaching practices, which in turn improve learning outcomes. By understanding how students interact with educational content and identifying where they struggle, educators can intervene more effectively, providing support exactly when and where it is needed. This data-driven approach to education is fundamentally reshaping how students learn, helping to create more engaging, personalized, and efficient educational experiences.

How Data is Reshaping Education

Data has become a powerful tool in transforming the educational landscape. With the rise of learning management systems, online education platforms, and adaptive learning technologies, vast amounts of data are being generated, collected, and analyzed in real time. This data can be anything from the number of attempts a student takes to complete a task to how much time they spend on each section of a lesson. The key to unlocking the potential of this data lies in learning informatics.

In a traditional classroom setting, teachers often rely on periodic assessments—like exams or quizzes—to gauge student understanding. However, this approach provides only a snapshot of student performance at a particular moment in time. Learning informatics, on the other hand, enables continuous data collection and analysis. This means that educators can monitor student progress on an ongoing basis, identifying trends and patterns that can help predict future performance or potential difficulties.

For example, if data analytics show that a group of students is consistently struggling with a particular concept, an instructor can take immediate action, such as offering additional resources or adjusting their teaching strategy. Similarly, data can reveal how different students learn best—whether through visual aids, interactive exercises, or traditional reading—allowing for more tailored and effective teaching methods.

Another significant impact of data in education is the shift toward personalized learning. Adaptive learning systems use data to adjust the pace, difficulty, and content of lessons based on individual student needs. For instance, if a student excels in a particular area, the system may present more advanced material to keep them challenged, while offering more foundational content to students who may need additional support. This personalized approach ensures that students receive the appropriate level of instruction, fostering better engagement and learning outcomes.

Data also plays a crucial role in educational assessment. Traditional assessments often focus on measuring knowledge retention through standardized testing, which may not always accurately reflect a student's understanding or learning process. By leveraging data analytics, educators can develop more nuanced assessments that consider not just the final answer, but also the process a student took to arrive at it. This can lead to more comprehensive evaluations that measure both cognitive development and critical thinking skills.

Moreover, data is helping institutions make informed decisions about curriculum development, resource allocation, and student support services. Schools and universities can use data insights to identify gaps in their programs, track long-term student performance trends, and make strategic decisions that improve overall educational quality.

In conclusion, data is reshaping education by enabling more personalized, adaptive, and continuous learning experiences. As learning informatics continues to evolve, the ability to harness data for educational improvement will only grow, offering exciting possibilities for the future of learning. Through the integration of data, technology, and human insight, education is becoming more efficient, inclusive, and responsive to the diverse needs of learners around the world.

Chapter 2: The Rise of Personalized Learning Systems

The rise of personalized learning systems is one of the most transformative developments in education today. These systems aim to tailor educational experiences to the needs, preferences, and pace of each learner, rather than relying on the traditional, one-size-fits-all model of instruction. Personalized learning leverages technology, data analytics, and adaptive learning platforms to create a customized educational journey, making learning more effective, engaging, and accessible for students of all backgrounds.

The Concept of Personalized Learning

Personalized learning refers to an educational approach that seeks to customize learning experiences to fit individual student needs. Instead of delivering uniform content to a group of students at the same time and pace, personalized learning adapts to the strengths, weaknesses, interests, and learning styles of each student. It allows for differentiated instruction, meaning students can focus on what they need to learn most, whether that's going deeper into topics they find interesting or receiving more support in areas where they are struggling.

At the core of personalized learning is the belief that every student is unique and learns at their own pace. Traditional education systems, which often rely on standard curricula and rigid timetables, can leave some students behind while others may find the material too easy and become disengaged. Personalized learning seeks to close this gap by offering a more flexible and student-centered approach.

There are several key principles that define personalized learning:

1. Learner-Centered: The student is at the center of the learning process, with the instruction tailored to their individual needs. This includes allowing students to have more control over their learning journey, including choosing certain topics or methods of study.

2. Flexibility: Students can move through the curriculum at their own pace, spending more time on challenging topics and less time on areas where they demonstrate mastery.

3. Data-Driven: Personalized learning relies heavily on data to track student progress and adapt to their evolving needs. This data can come from assessments, quizzes, or even real-time analytics of how students interact with learning materials.

4. Adaptive: The system dynamically adjusts content delivery based on student performance. If a student struggles with a specific concept, the platform may offer additional resources or simpler explanations before moving on.

5. Goal-Oriented: Students are often more motivated when they have a clear sense of their learning objectives. Personalized learning helps students set individual goals and provides them with the tools and pathways to achieve those goals.

While personalized learning can take many forms, its ultimate aim is to create a more engaging and effective educational experience by recognizing that no two students are alike. The rise of technology and data analytics has made it easier than ever to implement personalized learning systems in both traditional and online classrooms.

Adaptive Learning Technologies

At the heart of personalized learning systems is adaptive learning technology. Adaptive learning refers to systems that use artificial intelligence (AI) and data analytics to adjust educational content in real time based on a student's performance. These technologies are designed to continually assess each learner's progress and modify the instruction accordingly.

One of the key advantages of adaptive learning is that it allows for continuous feedback. Rather than waiting for the results of a formal assessment, adaptive systems provide immediate responses to student actions. For example, if a student answers a question incorrectly, the system can instantly offer additional explanations or simplify the concept before moving on to the next topic. Similarly, if a student demonstrates a deep understanding of a subject, the platform can present more advanced material to challenge them.

Several types of adaptive learning technologies are reshaping the educational landscape:

1. AI-Powered Platforms: These platforms use machine learning algorithms to monitor student behavior and predict what kind of learning materials will be most effective. Examples include systems that adapt the difficulty of questions based on previous answers or recommend personalized study paths based on a student's performance data.

2. Content Recommendation Systems: Similar to how streaming services like Netflix recommend content based on viewing habits, some adaptive learning platforms suggest learning resources based on a student's preferences and needs. This might

involve recommending videos, articles, or interactive exercises that align with a learner's unique challenges or interests.

3. Intelligent Tutoring Systems: These systems act as virtual tutors, guiding students through learning activities and providing immediate feedback. They can analyze student responses and adapt their instruction in real-time, offering personalized hints, examples, and alternative explanations.

4. Learning Analytics Dashboards: Many adaptive platforms offer educators and learners detailed dashboards that display progress, strengths, and areas needing improvement. These dashboards help students take ownership of their learning journey, while also providing teachers with insights to tailor instruction or provide targeted support.

The implementation of adaptive learning technologies has proven especially beneficial in large classrooms or online courses where individual attention from teachers may be limited. These technologies allow for a more personalized learning experience at scale, making it possible for teachers to meet the diverse needs of their students without having to modify their entire curriculum manually.

Case Studies: Successful Implementation of Personalized Learning

The success of personalized learning systems has been demonstrated in various educational settings, from K-12 schools to universities and corporate training programs. Below are a few case studies that highlight the transformative impact of personalized learning.

Case Study 1: Khan Academy

Khan Academy, an online learning platform offering free educational resources, has been a pioneer in personalized learning. The platform uses adaptive learning technology to tailor the educational experience to each student. As learners progress through a course, the platform adjusts the content based on their performance, ensuring that students only move on to new material once they've demonstrated mastery of the previous topics.

In 2014, a study by the SRI International found that students using Khan Academy's personalized learning tools performed significantly better in mathematics than those in traditional classroom settings. The ability to learn at their own pace and receive instant feedback helped students improve their understanding of complex mathematical concepts. The platform's data-driven approach also provided teachers with insights into student progress, allowing for more targeted interventions when needed.

Case Study 2: Summit Learning Program

Summit Learning is a personalized learning program that has been implemented in numerous K-12 schools across the United States. The program focuses on student agency, allowing learners to set their own goals and manage their learning journey with the support of teachers and mentors. The platform uses data to track student progress, offering a customized curriculum that adapts to each student's pace and level of understanding.

Research on the Summit Learning Program has shown that students who participate in personalized learning environments demonstrate higher levels of engagement and improved academic performance. A 2019 study conducted by RAND Corporation found that schools using the Summit Learning model saw better outcomes in terms of student growth, particularly among disadvantaged students who typically struggle in traditional educational settings.

Case Study 3: McGraw-Hill's ALEKS

ALEKS (Assessment and Learning in Knowledge Spaces) is an adaptive learning platform used in higher education, particularly in math and science courses. The system assesses students' knowledge levels and tailors the learning experience to their individual needs. By continuously analyzing student performance, ALEKS identifies gaps in understanding and provides customized learning paths to address those gaps.

A 2018 study at Arizona State University found that students using ALEKS in math courses demonstrated higher retention rates and better performance compared to students in non-adaptive learning environments. The platform's ability to provide personalized content and immediate feedback helped students overcome learning obstacles more quickly and effectively.

Conclusion

The rise of personalized learning systems marks a fundamental shift in how education is delivered. Through adaptive learning technologies and data-driven platforms, education is becoming more tailored, flexible, and responsive to the unique needs of each learner. Whether in primary education, higher education, or corporate training, personalized learning systems are providing students with more engaging and effective learning experiences. As technology continues to evolve, the possibilities for further personalizing education will only expand, promising a future where every student can achieve their full potential through customized learning pathways.

Chapter 3: Learning Management Systems (LMS) and Online Education Platforms

---

In today's increasingly digital educational landscape, Learning Management Systems (LMS) and online education platforms have become central to delivering, managing, and optimizing educational experiences. These systems are designed to facilitate the organization, delivery, and tracking of educational content, whether for schools, universities, or corporate training programs. With the rise of remote learning, LMS platforms are playing an even more critical role in ensuring access to quality education for students regardless of their location.

Overview of Popular LMS Platforms

Over the past few years, several LMS platforms have emerged as leaders in the field of online education. These platforms offer a wide range of tools and features that enable educational institutions, corporations, and individual educators to create, manage, and track learning experiences. Below is an overview of some of the most popular LMS platforms in use today:

1. Moodle

Moodle is one of the most widely used open-source LMS platforms in the world. Its flexibility and customization options make it a favorite among educators and institutions looking for a free and adaptable platform. Moodle allows educators to create courses, assign assessments, track student progress, and provide feedback. Because it's open-source, users can customize it extensively to meet their specific needs.

Moodle's strong community support and continuous updates make it a reliable choice for institutions looking to implement LMS solutions on a budget. It has a variety of plugins that expand its functionality, such as interactive learning tools, social learning features, and gamified elements, providing a highly versatile environment.

2. Canvas

Canvas, developed by Instructure, is a cloud-based LMS that is particularly popular in higher education. It offers a user-friendly interface and robust features, including integrations with third-party apps, a mobile app for learning on the go, and strong analytics tools. Canvas is known for its ease of use for both instructors and students, making course creation, grading, and communication simple and intuitive.

In addition, Canvas has strong collaboration tools, enabling students and educators to work together through discussion forums, group projects, and peer reviews. This interactivity supports dynamic learning environments, making it a favored choice among many colleges and universities.

3. Blackboard

Blackboard has been a longstanding player in the LMS market, particularly in higher education. Known for its comprehensive suite of tools, Blackboard provides course management, virtual classrooms, assessments, and robust analytics for tracking student engagement and performance. Instructors can create customized learning paths for students, integrate multimedia content, and conduct assessments directly within the platform.

Blackboard's strength lies in its advanced features for administrative control, making it an ideal choice for large institutions needing centralized management of multiple courses. Its versatility, coupled with its strong support network, has kept it relevant even in the face of newer LMS competitors.

4. Google Classroom

Google Classroom, part of the Google Workspace for Education, is a simple and efficient LMS that integrates seamlessly with other Google services such as Google Drive, Docs, Sheets, and Meet. It is widely used in K-12 education but has also found success in higher education and professional training environments due to its simplicity and integration with Google's widely used suite of tools.

Google Classroom allows educators to create and distribute assignments, provide real-time feedback, and communicate with students. Its intuitive interface and ease of use make it ideal for educators who may not be tech-savvy but still need a digital tool to manage their classes.

5. Edmodo

Edmodo is a social learning platform designed to connect students, teachers, and parents. With a focus on collaboration and communication, Edmodo provides a safe online environment for educational discussions, assignments, and resource sharing. Its user-friendly design and focus on K-12 education make it a go-to platform for schools looking to implement a straightforward LMS solution.

Unlike some of the more complex LMS platforms, Edmodo emphasizes engagement and social learning, making it a popular choice for teachers who want to foster interactive and collaborative learning environments.

Features and Functions of Modern LMS

Modern Learning Management Systems are much more than platforms for delivering content—they are comprehensive ecosystems that support teaching, learning, and administration. Here are some of the key features and functions of today's LMS platforms:

1. Course Creation and Management

At its core, an LMS provides the tools for creating, delivering, and managing educational courses. Instructors can upload course materials such as readings, videos, and quizzes, organize them into modules, and manage assessments. Many LMS platforms offer drag-and-drop interfaces that make course creation simple and flexible.

2. Assessments and Grading

LMS platforms allow educators to create a variety of assessments, including quizzes, exams, essays, and projects. Many systems provide automatic grading for multiple-choice or true/false questions, while instructors can manually grade more subjective assessments like essays. LMS platforms also offer tools for tracking student progress and generating reports on their performance.

3. Analytics and Reporting

One of the most powerful features of modern LMS platforms is their ability to collect and analyze data on student performance. This includes tracking engagement metrics such as login frequency, time spent on tasks, and completion rates. The analytics tools provide insights that can help educators identify students who may be struggling and offer targeted support to improve their learning outcomes.

4. Communication and Collaboration

LMS platforms facilitate communication between students and educators through discussion forums, messaging systems, and live chat features. Many platforms also offer tools for collaborative learning, such as group projects, peer review systems, and shared workspaces where students can work together in real-time.

5. Mobile Accessibility

As more students access learning materials from their smartphones or tablets, mobile compatibility has become an essential feature of LMS platforms. Many systems now offer dedicated mobile apps that allow students to access course content, participate in discussions, submit assignments, and even take quizzes directly from their mobile devices.

6. Integrations with Third-Party Tools

LMS platforms are increasingly integrating with other software and tools to create a more seamless learning experience. This might include video conferencing tools like Zoom, content creation tools like Adobe Creative Cloud, and productivity tools like Slack or Microsoft Teams. These integrations enhance the functionality of the LMS, making it a comprehensive hub for all aspects of online learning.

The Impact of LMS on Remote Learning

The advent of Learning Management Systems has been particularly impactful in the context of remote learning. As educational institutions around the world transitioned to online learning due to the COVID-19 pandemic, LMS platforms became critical for delivering education to students who could no longer attend physical classrooms. Below are some of the ways in which LMS platforms have transformed remote learning:

1. Increased Accessibility

One of the most significant benefits of LMS platforms is their ability to make education more accessible. Students no longer need to be physically present in a classroom to receive instruction—they can access lectures, assignments, and resources from anywhere in the world as long as they have an internet connection. This has opened up educational opportunities for students in rural or underserved areas who may not have access to high-quality educational institutions.

2. Flexibility in Learning

LMS platforms offer greater flexibility in how students engage with their education. Unlike traditional classroom environments where students must attend lectures at a specific time, LMS platforms allow students to learn at their own pace. This flexibility is particularly beneficial for adult learners or students who may have other commitments, such as work or family responsibilities.

3. Enhanced Engagement

LMS platforms offer a variety of tools that help keep students engaged in their learning, even in remote environments. Features like discussion forums, interactive quizzes, and gamification elements make learning more interactive and enjoyable. Some LMS platforms also offer virtual classrooms, where students can participate in live discussions or watch recorded lectures.

4. Personalized Learning Paths

As discussed in the previous chapter, many modern LMS platforms offer adaptive learning features that personalize the learning experience based on individual student performance. This level of personalization is particularly important in remote learning environments, where students may feel disconnected from their peers or instructors. By offering tailored learning paths, LMS platforms can help ensure that students remain engaged and motivated, even when learning remotely.

5. Continuous Feedback and Support

LMS platforms provide students with continuous feedback on their performance through quizzes, assessments, and progress reports. This immediate feedback helps students understand where they need to improve and keeps them motivated to continue learning. Additionally, LMS platforms often include tools for communication between students and instructors, ensuring that students can receive support when needed, even outside of normal classroom hours.

Conclusion

Learning Management Systems and online education platforms have fundamentally changed how education is delivered and experienced. By offering flexibility, accessibility, and personalization, these platforms enable educators to create dynamic, engaging learning environments that meet the needs of today's students. As technology continues to evolve, the role of LMS platforms in education is likely to grow even further, making them an essential component of modern learning. Whether in traditional classrooms or remote learning environments, LMS platforms are helping to shape the future of education by making it more inclusive, effective, and adaptive to the needs of individual learners.

Chapter 4: Gamification in Education

In the quest to enhance student engagement and motivation, educators and technologists have increasingly turned to gamification as a powerful tool. Gamification, or the application of game-design elements in non-game contexts, is transforming education by creating dynamic, interactive, and rewarding learning experiences. By incorporating elements such as point systems, badges, leaderboards, and challenges, gamification can make learning more enjoyable and engaging for students. This chapter explores the principles of gamification, the use of virtual learning environments (VLEs) in education, and how gamification enhances student engagement and motivation.

The Principles of Gamification

At its core, gamification is about applying the principles of game design to educational contexts. These principles aim to leverage the intrinsic motivations that make games so appealing—such as competition, achievement, and reward—to enhance learning. Below are some key principles of gamification and how they are applied in education:

1. Progress and Achievement

One of the key principles of gamification is the use of clear goals and progress indicators. In games, players are often motivated by the prospect of completing levels, unlocking achievements, or earning rewards. This same principle can be applied to education by setting clear learning objectives and providing students with a way to track their progress toward achieving them.

For instance, in a gamified classroom, students might earn points or badges for completing assignments, participating in discussions, or mastering new concepts. These achievements serve as milestones that not only provide a sense of accomplishment but also keep students motivated to continue engaging with the material.

2. Immediate Feedback

Games provide players with instant feedback on their actions, allowing them to adjust their strategies and improve their performance. In an educational context, this principle can be applied by offering students immediate feedback on their work, whether through automated quizzes, peer reviews, or instructor comments.

Immediate feedback helps students understand where they are excelling and where they need to improve, fostering a more iterative and reflective learning process. This instant reinforcement, often seen in video games, helps sustain engagement and encourages students to try again, much like retrying a game level.

3. Competition and Collaboration

Games often involve elements of competition, either against other players or against the game itself. In education, competition can be used to motivate students to improve their performance by introducing leaderboards or friendly contests. For example, students might compete to earn the most points in a class-wide quiz, with the highest scorers recognized in front of their peers.

However, collaboration is also a vital principle in gamification. Many games require players to work together to achieve shared goals, and this collaborative approach can be applied in educational settings to foster teamwork and peer learning. Group challenges, cooperative problem-solving tasks, and shared learning objectives can encourage students to collaborate while still benefiting from the motivational aspects of gamification.

4. Levels and Challenges

Games typically present players with increasingly difficult challenges as they progress, keeping them engaged and motivated. Similarly, in a gamified educational environment, students can be presented with progressively harder tasks as they master the basics. By breaking down complex concepts into manageable steps, educators can maintain student interest while gradually building their skills and knowledge.

This concept of "leveling up" can be incorporated into course design by organizing content into tiers of difficulty, with students needing to master each tier before advancing to the next. This creates a structured, yet dynamic learning experience that mirrors the progression systems found in games.

5. Rewards and Recognition

Rewards are a significant part of what makes games so engaging. In education, rewards can come in many forms, from points and badges to certificates and public recognition. These rewards provide students with tangible evidence of their accomplishments, reinforcing their motivation to continue learning.

The concept of "extrinsic rewards" (such as badges or points) can complement "intrinsic rewards" (such as the satisfaction of mastering a skill). Over time, students who initially engage in a gamified learning environment for the extrinsic rewards may find themselves becoming more intrinsically motivated, as they take greater pride in their achievements and personal growth.

Virtual Learning Environments and Their Educational Benefits

Virtual Learning Environments (VLEs) are digital platforms that allow students to engage with educational content in immersive and interactive ways. VLEs often incorporate elements of gamification to make learning more engaging and accessible, offering a variety of tools and features that simulate the experience of being in a classroom, but with added layers of interaction, visualization, and feedback.

1. Interactive Simulations and Real-World Applications

VLEs enable students to interact with complex simulations that mimic real-world scenarios, which can enhance their understanding of theoretical concepts. For example, in science education, students might use a VLE to conduct virtual chemistry experiments, allowing them to manipulate variables and observe the outcomes without the need for physical lab equipment. These simulations are not only safer and more cost-effective but also allow for repeated trials, giving students the freedom to experiment without fear of failure.

Incorporating gamification into these simulations, such as setting specific challenges or giving students rewards for completing tasks, can make the learning process more interactive and goal-oriented. This encourages students to apply critical thinking and problem-solving skills in a low-risk environment where they can learn from their mistakes.

2. Collaborative Learning Spaces

Many VLEs feature collaborative spaces where students can work together on group projects or engage in discussions. Gamification elements, such as team-based challenges or group quests, can be used within these spaces to promote collaboration and foster a sense of community. These collaborative environments help students learn from their peers, develop communication skills, and feel more connected to their learning experience, even in a virtual setting.

Virtual worlds, such as those found in platforms like Minecraft Education or Second Life, allow students to interact with each other in gamified spaces, working together to solve problems, build structures, or explore digital landscapes. These types of collaborative, interactive learning experiences help students develop critical skills while enjoying the immersive benefits of a game-like environment.

3. Flexible Learning Paths and Adaptive Content

One of the key benefits of VLEs is their ability to provide personalized learning paths for students. By incorporating adaptive learning technologies, VLEs can adjust the content and difficulty of tasks based on individual student performance. This creates a more tailored learning experience that caters to each student's strengths and areas for improvement.

Gamification enhances this process by rewarding students as they progress through their learning journey. For instance, students might receive points, badges, or new "levels" as they complete various tasks, encouraging them to continue advancing through the content at their own pace. This flexibility empowers students to take control of their learning while still feeling supported and motivated by the system's feedback mechanisms.

How Gamification Enhances Student Engagement and Motivation

Gamification has been shown to significantly boost student engagement and motivation by making learning more interactive, rewarding, and enjoyable. Here are some of the ways in which gamification positively impacts students:

1. Increased Engagement Through Interactivity

Traditional educational approaches can sometimes lead to passive learning, where students are expected to absorb information without much active involvement. Gamification changes this by encouraging students to actively participate in their learning. Through interactive elements like quizzes, games, and challenges, students become more engaged in the material, increasing their focus and retention.

By introducing game-like mechanics, such as time-bound challenges or competitive quizzes, students are motivated to actively engage with the content, turning passive learning into an interactive and rewarding experience.

2. Boosting Motivation with Rewards

Students are naturally motivated by rewards, whether those rewards are tangible (points, badges) or intangible (recognition, progress). Gamification taps into this motivation by providing students with frequent, visible rewards that acknowledge their efforts. This creates a positive feedback loop, where students are encouraged to continue engaging with the material in order to earn more rewards.

Moreover, the sense of accomplishment that comes with unlocking new achievements or advancing to a higher level can provide a significant boost to a student's self-confidence, further motivating them to pursue their learning goals.

3. Encouraging Perseverance and Resilience

One of the key benefits of gamification is that it encourages students to persist in the face of challenges. In games, players often encounter difficult levels or challenges that require multiple attempts to overcome. This same principle can be applied to education: by framing difficult tasks as "challenges" to be overcome, students are more likely to persevere through setbacks, viewing them as opportunities for growth rather than failures.

Additionally, the frequent feedback provided by gamified systems helps students learn from their mistakes and try again, fostering a growth mindset. This ability to bounce back from challenges is a crucial skill in both academic settings and life.

4. Making Learning Fun and Enjoyable

Ultimately, one of the greatest strengths of gamification is that it makes learning fun. By incorporating elements of play into the learning process, educators can create a more enjoyable and engaging environment. When students associate learning with fun, they are more likely to approach it with enthusiasm and curiosity, leading to deeper and more meaningful engagement with the material.

Conclusion

Gamification has the potential to revolutionize the educational landscape by making learning more interactive, engaging, and rewarding. By applying the principles of game design to education, educators can create dynamic, motivating environments that encourage students to take an active role in their learning. Whether through the use of virtual learning environments, personalized learning paths, or reward systems, gamification is helping to create a more enjoyable and effective learning experience for students around the world. As education continues to evolve in the digital age, the use of gamification will likely play an even greater role in shaping the future of learning.

Chapter 5: Data Analytics in Educational Assessment

In today's increasingly digital educational landscape, data analytics has become a critical tool in assessing student performance, improving learning outcomes, and providing personalized education. By collecting, analyzing, and interpreting vast amounts of data, educators and institutions can gain deep insights into student behavior, learning patterns, and areas of improvement. Educational data analytics not only enables more effective teaching strategies but also helps students to better understand their own learning journeys through real-time feedback systems.

This chapter delves into the concepts of educational data analytics, exploring how data-driven assessments enhance learning outcomes and how real-time analytics and feedback systems are transforming the way students are assessed.

Understanding Educational Data Analytics

Educational data analytics involves the systematic use of data to evaluate and improve learning processes. By analyzing data from a variety of sources—such as test results, student interactions with digital platforms, attendance records, and engagement metrics—educators can identify patterns, predict outcomes, and create targeted interventions that enhance the educational experience.

1. Types of Data Collected in Education

Educational data analytics draws on both qualitative and quantitative data, collected from various educational tools and platforms. Here are some common types of data used:

- Assessment Scores: These include traditional test results, quizzes, and other forms of formal assessments that help measure student knowledge and skills.

- Behavioral Data: This type of data captures how students interact with learning platforms, such as their participation in discussions, time spent on assignments, and frequency of login activities.

- Engagement Metrics: These data points include student engagement levels in activities like video tutorials, interactive simulations, and collaborative projects.

- Attendance and Participation: The data reflecting student attendance in physical or virtual classrooms and their participation in group work or online forums can offer insights into student involvement.

- Demographic Data: Personal information such as age, background, and learning preferences, which helps to tailor learning experiences for specific student groups.

- Learning Pathways: This data shows the learning progression of students, identifying the areas where they excel or struggle, allowing for personalized feedback and support.

2. The Role of Big Data in Education

With the proliferation of digital learning platforms and tools, the amount of educational data available has grown exponentially. This has given rise to the use of big data analytics in education, where large volumes of structured and unstructured data are analyzed to uncover trends and insights. Big data allows educators and institutions to go beyond simple assessment scores and look at broader patterns of learning and behavior across entire student populations.

For example, big data can be used to determine which teaching methods are most effective for different types of learners, or to predict which students are at risk of falling behind based on their engagement patterns. The sheer volume of data generated in educational settings offers a unique opportunity to continuously improve learning outcomes through informed decision-making.

How Data-Driven Assessments Improve Learning Outcomes

Data-driven assessments leverage the insights derived from educational data to enhance teaching methodologies, personalize learning experiences, and ultimately improve student outcomes. By identifying areas of strength and weakness, data analytics allows for more targeted interventions that help students achieve their full potential.

1. Personalized Learning Pathways

One of the key benefits of data-driven assessments is the ability to create personalized learning pathways for students. Traditional education systems often use a one-size-fits-all approach, where all students are taught the same material at the same pace. However, not all students learn in the same way or at the same speed, leading to disengagement or frustration among some learners.

Through data analytics, educators can tailor learning experiences to the needs of each student. For instance, if data shows that a student is struggling with a particular concept, the system can automatically adjust the difficulty of the content or provide additional resources, such as tutorials or practice exercises. Similarly, students who excel in certain areas can be offered more advanced material to keep them challenged and engaged.

This personalized approach ensures that students receive the support they need in real-time, which improves their overall learning experience and helps them to progress at their own pace.

2. Early Intervention and Predictive Analytics

Data analytics also enables predictive modeling, which can be used to identify students who may be at risk of academic failure. By analyzing factors such as attendance, engagement, and performance trends, predictive analytics can alert educators to potential issues before they become significant problems.

For example, if a student consistently scores low on quizzes or shows a pattern of disengagement, the system can flag this for the teacher, allowing them to intervene early. This might involve offering the student additional tutoring, providing more interactive learning materials, or even reaching out to parents to discuss potential support strategies.

Early intervention based on data insights can dramatically improve a student's chances of success, preventing them from falling too far behind and giving them the tools they need to catch up.

3. Data-Driven Feedback and Self-Assessment

In addition to helping educators, data-driven assessments also benefit students by offering personalized feedback on their performance. By providing data-based insights into their learning progress, students can gain a better understanding of their strengths and weaknesses.

For instance, students can receive detailed reports that show their performance over time, including areas where they have improved and concepts that may require further review. This kind of feedback allows students to take ownership of their learning and make informed decisions about how to allocate their study time.

Moreover, data-driven self-assessment tools can help students reflect on their own progress. Many learning platforms now include features that allow students to set personal goals, track their achievements, and see how they compare to their peers. This kind of self-awareness encourages a growth mindset, where students are motivated to continuously improve and strive for academic success.

Real-Time Analytics and Feedback Systems

One of the most powerful applications of data analytics in education is the use of real-time analytics and feedback systems. Unlike traditional assessments that only offer feedback after a test or assignment is completed, real-time analytics provide instant insights into student performance, allowing for immediate adjustments to the learning process.

1. Instant Feedback for Students

Real-time feedback systems enable students to receive instant feedback on their work, whether they are taking an online quiz, completing a practice exercise, or participating in a group project. This immediate feedback helps students understand where they went wrong and allows them to correct their mistakes on the spot.

For example, in an online math course, a student might receive immediate feedback after solving a problem, letting them know if their answer is correct or not. If they get the answer wrong, the system might offer hints or explanations, guiding them toward the correct solution. This kind of immediate correction helps to reinforce learning in the moment, making it more effective than delayed feedback.

2. Real-Time Monitoring for Educators

Educators can also benefit from real-time analytics by monitoring student performance and engagement during class activities. This allows teachers to identify students who may be struggling in real-time and provide targeted support when needed.

For instance, if an educator notices that a significant portion of the class is performing poorly on a particular concept during an online activity, they can pause the lesson to review the material, offer additional explanations, or modify the approach. Real-time analytics can even highlight specific students who may need extra attention, allowing educators to offer one-on-one support during or after class.

This real-time monitoring helps educators stay proactive in addressing learning challenges, rather than waiting until formal assessments are completed to intervene.

3. Adaptive Learning Powered by Real-Time Data

Another exciting application of real-time analytics is in adaptive learning systems, where the content and difficulty of tasks are dynamically adjusted based on student performance. These systems use real-time data to continuously assess a student's progress and adjust the learning pathway accordingly.

For example, if a student is performing exceptionally well on a series of math problems, the system may offer more challenging questions to keep them engaged. Conversely, if the student is struggling, the system might simplify the problems or provide additional resources to help them grasp the concept. This adaptive approach ensures that students are always working at the right level of difficulty, maximizing their learning potential.

Conclusion

Data analytics is transforming educational assessment by providing educators with the tools to create personalized learning experiences, offer real-time feedback, and intervene early when students need support. By leveraging the power of big data, predictive analytics, and adaptive learning systems, educational institutions can improve student outcomes and create more effective learning environments. As technology continues to evolve, the role of data analytics in education will only grow, offering even more opportunities to enhance teaching and learning in innovative and impactful ways.

Chapter 6:

Virtual Classrooms and Remote Learning Tools

The COVID-19 pandemic dramatically reshaped the global education landscape, accelerating the adoption of virtual classrooms and remote learning tools at an unprecedented rate. In the face of widespread school closures and social distancing mandates, educators and institutions were forced to quickly pivot to online platforms to maintain continuity in learning. What was initially seen as a temporary solution has evolved into a long-term shift in how education is delivered, with virtual classrooms becoming an integral part of the educational ecosystem.

In this chapter, we explore the growth of virtual classrooms post-COVID-19, the best practices for implementing effective virtual learning, and how remote education is poised to shape the future of learning.

The Growth of Virtual Classrooms Post-COVID-19

1. The Pandemic's Impact on Education

The onset of the COVID-19 pandemic in early 2020 led to a massive disruption in education. Schools, colleges, and universities around the world were forced to close their doors, leaving millions of students without access to traditional, in-person instruction. In response, educational institutions turned to technology to fill the gap, leveraging virtual classrooms and online learning platforms to ensure that learning could continue in the midst of the crisis.

During this period, virtual learning tools—such as video conferencing software (e.g., Zoom, Microsoft Teams, Google Meet), learning management systems (LMS), and interactive digital tools—became the primary means of delivering education. The shift to remote learning, which once seemed like a temporary fix, has since become a permanent and growing aspect of education.

Virtual classrooms offer a flexible, scalable, and accessible solution for both students and educators, making it possible to teach and learn from anywhere in the world. This mode of learning has also opened doors for students who may have previously faced barriers to accessing quality education, such as those living in remote areas or individuals with disabilities.

2. Permanent Shifts in Education

While in-person learning remains essential in many contexts, the rise of virtual classrooms during the pandemic has shown that remote education can be just as effective, if not more so, when implemented correctly. Many institutions have adopted a hybrid model of learning, combining the strengths of both in-person and virtual classrooms to provide students with more diverse and flexible learning experiences.

Moreover, virtual classrooms have facilitated global collaboration, where students and educators from different countries can connect and share knowledge without the constraints of physical proximity. This has given rise to a more interconnected, global education system.

Best Practices for Implementing Virtual Learning

To fully realize the benefits of virtual classrooms and remote learning tools, educators must adopt best practices that ensure students remain engaged, motivated, and supported. Virtual learning environments present unique challenges—such as reduced face-to-face interaction, potential distractions, and technical issues—that require thoughtful planning and execution. Here are some best practices for implementing virtual learning effectively:

1. Establish Clear Expectations and Guidelines

One of the key factors in ensuring a successful virtual classroom is setting clear expectations from the outset. Educators should communicate with students about how the virtual classroom will operate, including guidelines on participation, attendance, behavior, and deadlines. Virtual learning environments require structure, and students must know what is expected of them, even though they are not physically present in a traditional classroom.

Clear communication helps to create a sense of accountability and encourages students to take their virtual learning experience as seriously as they would in-person classes.

2. Leverage Interactive Tools to Promote Engagement

Engagement is one of the biggest challenges in virtual classrooms. Without the physical presence of peers and teachers, students may find it difficult to stay focused and motivated. To address this issue, educators should use interactive tools that promote active participation, collaboration, and engagement.

Some examples of interactive tools include:

- Polls and Quizzes: Quick polls or quizzes during lessons help to maintain student attention and encourage participation.

- Breakout Rooms: Virtual platforms like Zoom and Microsoft Teams offer breakout room features that allow students to work in smaller groups, fostering collaboration and discussion.
- Discussion Forums: Asynchronous discussion forums provide students with a platform to share their thoughts, ask questions, and engage with their peers and instructors outside of live sessions.
- Gamification: Incorporating game-like elements such as badges, rewards, or competition can make learning more fun and engaging for students.

3. Provide Ongoing Support and Feedback

In a virtual classroom, students may feel isolated or disconnected from their instructors and peers. To combat this, it is important for educators to maintain regular communication and provide ongoing support to ensure students feel engaged and supported in their learning journey.

Regular check-ins, office hours, and personalized feedback can help bridge the gap between the virtual and physical classroom, making students feel more connected and valued. Additionally, educators should encourage students to reach out if they need assistance or clarification on course materials.

4. Use Multiple Modes of Instruction

To cater to different learning styles, educators should use a variety of instructional methods in virtual classrooms. This might include live video lectures, pre-recorded lessons, reading materials, interactive exercises, and multimedia content such as videos or infographics. The use of diverse instructional materials ensures that students have multiple avenues to understand and engage with the course content.

Moreover, the use of asynchronous content, such as recorded lectures and readings, allows students to learn at their own pace, which is a significant advantage in remote learning environments.

5. Promote Collaboration and Peer Interaction

Virtual classrooms should not be a solitary experience. Fostering collaboration and peer interaction is essential for creating a sense of community and enhancing the learning experience. Group projects, peer reviews, and collaborative discussions can help students stay connected with one another and encourage the exchange of ideas.

Collaborative tools like Google Docs, shared online workspaces, and group chat features in LMS platforms can be used to facilitate teamwork and ensure that students are working together, even when they are physically apart.

The Future of Remote Education

The shift to virtual classrooms and remote learning is not a temporary phenomenon. In fact, the future of education is likely to be shaped by an increasing reliance on digital tools, online platforms, and remote learning environments. Several key trends will continue to influence the evolution of remote education:

1. Blended Learning Models

As the education sector continues to evolve, hybrid or blended learning models are becoming more popular. Blended learning combines traditional, in-person instruction with online learning, offering students the flexibility to choose how they engage with course materials. This model allows institutions to leverage the benefits of both physical and virtual learning environments, ensuring that students have a more comprehensive and personalized educational experience.

For example, students may attend in-person lectures for certain subjects while completing online assignments and participating in virtual discussions for others. This flexibility makes education more accessible to a wider range of learners, particularly those with other commitments such as work or family.

2. Artificial Intelligence (AI) and Machine Learning

AI and machine learning are poised to play an increasingly significant role in the future of remote education. These technologies have the potential to create highly personalized learning experiences by analyzing student data and adapting course materials to meet individual needs. AI-powered tutoring systems, intelligent feedback tools, and adaptive learning platforms are already being used to enhance remote education.

For instance, AI-driven platforms can monitor student performance in real-time and provide tailored resources or interventions when students are struggling with particular concepts. This personalized support helps to bridge the gap between traditional and remote education, ensuring that students receive the assistance they need to succeed.

3. The Rise of Virtual and Augmented Reality

Virtual reality (VR) and augmented reality (AR) technologies are set to transform the way students engage with remote learning. These immersive technologies have the potential to create virtual learning environments that replicate or enhance in-person experiences. For example, medical students can use VR to practice surgical procedures in a virtual operating room, or history students can take virtual tours of ancient civilizations.

As VR and AR technologies continue to improve and become more affordable, they will offer new and exciting ways for students to learn and engage with content in remote education settings.

4. Global Learning Communities

One of the most profound impacts of remote education is its ability to create global learning communities. In a virtual classroom, students and educators from different parts of the world can come together to share ideas, perspectives, and knowledge. This global exchange of ideas enriches the learning experience and helps students develop a broader understanding of the world.

Virtual classrooms have broken down geographic barriers, making it possible for students to access top-quality education from anywhere. As this trend continues, remote education will contribute to a more interconnected and diverse global education system.

Conclusion

Virtual classrooms and remote learning tools have revolutionized the way education is delivered, offering new opportunities for flexibility, accessibility, and innovation. As technology continues to evolve, so too will the tools and platforms that support remote education, paving the way for a future where learning is no longer bound by physical classrooms or geographic limitations. By embracing best practices and staying attuned to emerging trends, educators can ensure that virtual classrooms remain a powerful and effective mode of learning in the years to come.

Chapter 7:

Adaptive Learning Systems and AI in Education

The rapid advancement of artificial intelligence (AI) in recent years has revolutionized numerous industries, and education is no exception. One of the most significant applications of AI in education is the development of adaptive learning systems. These systems leverage AI algorithms to create personalized, dynamic learning experiences that adjust to each student's unique needs, abilities, and learning pace. The promise of adaptive learning lies in its potential to enhance the traditional one-size-fits-all education model by offering a tailored, data-driven approach that improves student outcomes and engagement.

In this chapter, we explore the role of AI in adaptive learning, the various AI-powered educational tools and resources that are shaping modern classrooms, and how AI is transforming the learning process by providing personalized, effective, and scalable education solutions.

The Role of Artificial Intelligence in Adaptive Learning

1. Understanding Adaptive Learning

Adaptive learning refers to educational systems that use data and algorithms to tailor learning experiences to individual students. Instead of following a rigid, predetermined curriculum, adaptive learning systems continuously assess a student's progress, identify areas where they need improvement, and adjust the content, pace, and difficulty level accordingly. This approach allows students to learn at their own pace, focusing on areas where they need the most help, while moving more quickly through concepts they have already mastered.

The core of adaptive learning is AI, which powers the algorithms and data analysis that make real-time adjustments possible. By analyzing vast amounts of data on student behavior, performance, and preferences, AI can predict the most effective learning paths for each individual and optimize instruction accordingly.

2. AI's Role in Personalized Education

Personalization is one of the most promising aspects of AI in education. Traditional classroom environments often struggle to meet the diverse needs of all students due to time constraints, class sizes, and standardized teaching methods. AI, however, enables personalized learning at scale. Adaptive learning systems powered by AI can tailor educational content to each student's strengths and weaknesses, providing a more individualized approach.

AI-driven adaptive learning systems analyze data points such as:

- Student performance: Exam results, quiz scores, and assignment outcomes help the system identify areas where a student is excelling or struggling.
- Learning behavior: Data on how students interact with learning materials—such as how long they spend on a particular concept, how often they revisit content, and how they engage with multimedia resources—can offer insights into their learning style.
- Engagement levels: By tracking engagement metrics, such as participation in discussions, completion rates, and attentiveness during lectures, AI can determine which teaching methods are most effective for each student.

With this information, AI-powered adaptive learning systems can adjust the curriculum dynamically, recommending supplementary materials, changing the difficulty level of questions, or suggesting alternative instructional approaches to improve comprehension.

3. AI's Predictive Capabilities in Education

One of the powerful features of AI in adaptive learning is its predictive capabilities. Based on patterns in a student's performance and behavior, AI algorithms can predict future outcomes and challenges. For example, if a student consistently struggles with certain types of problems, the system can predict that they might have difficulty with upcoming topics and provide preemptive support or extra practice.

AI can also help identify at-risk students who may be falling behind and intervene before they encounter significant difficulties. By detecting early warning signs—such as a drop in engagement or a decline in performance—AI systems can alert educators and offer personalized remediation strategies to help the student get back on track.

AI-Powered Educational Tools and Resources

The integration of AI into education has led to the development of a wide range of tools and resources that support adaptive learning. These tools are designed to enhance the learning experience by offering personalized support, automating administrative tasks, and improving the efficiency of teaching and learning processes.

1. Intelligent Tutoring Systems (ITS)

One of the most notable applications of AI in education is the development of intelligent tutoring systems (ITS). These systems provide personalized tutoring and feedback to students, mimicking the experience of working with a one-on-one human tutor. Intelligent tutoring systems use AI to assess a student's understanding of a topic, guide them through learning activities, and provide real-time feedback.

For example, platforms like Carnegie Learning's MATHia use AI-powered tutors to help students master mathematical concepts. The system adapts the difficulty and type of problems based on the student's performance, providing hints, explanations, and practice problems when needed.

2. AI-Powered Learning Management Systems (LMS)

Learning management systems (LMS) are widely used in both K-12 and higher education to organize and deliver online courses. With the integration of AI, modern LMS platforms have become more sophisticated, offering personalized learning experiences through adaptive learning modules.

AI-powered LMS platforms, such as Knewton and Smart Sparrow, analyze student data to provide personalized recommendations for study materials, assignments, and assessments. These systems can also automate administrative tasks, such as grading and tracking student progress, allowing educators to focus more on instruction and student support.

3. Automated Grading and Feedback

AI-powered tools are increasingly being used to automate grading and provide immediate feedback to students. While traditional grading methods can be time-consuming and inconsistent, AI algorithms can evaluate assignments, quizzes, and even essays in real-time, providing instant feedback.

For example, platforms like Gradescope use AI to assist teachers in grading by identifying patterns in student responses and categorizing similar answers. This allows for faster grading of large classes and provides students with timely feedback on their work.

AI-driven feedback systems also offer personalized insights. For instance, if a student consistently makes the same type of mistake, the system can provide targeted feedback and suggest resources to address that specific issue.

4. AI Chatbots for Student Support

AI-powered chatbots are becoming popular in educational settings, providing students with instant support and answers to frequently asked questions. These chatbots can assist with administrative tasks, such as answering questions about course schedules, assignments, and deadlines, freeing up educators and support staff to focus on more complex tasks.

For example, Georgia State University implemented an AI chatbot called Pounce to help students navigate the admissions process, answer questions about financial aid, and provide reminders about important deadlines. The chatbot significantly reduced student attrition rates by ensuring students had the information and support they needed to stay enrolled.

How AI is Transforming the Learning Process

The impact of AI on the learning process is profound. By enhancing personalization, automating tasks, and providing real-time data analysis, AI is transforming the way students learn and educators teach. Here are several key ways AI is reshaping the learning process:

1. Personalized Learning at Scale

One of the biggest challenges in traditional education is addressing the diverse needs of students within a single classroom. AI-powered adaptive learning systems solve this problem by enabling personalized learning at scale. These systems can cater to thousands of students simultaneously, offering individualized content, feedback, and support without the need for additional human resources.

This scalability allows institutions to provide high-quality education to a larger and more diverse student population, ensuring that every student receives the attention and resources they need to succeed.

2. Real-Time Data and Insights

AI's ability to analyze data in real-time has a significant impact on the learning process. Educators can access detailed insights into student performance, engagement, and behavior, allowing them to make data-driven decisions about how to support individual learners.

For example, if an educator notices that a group of students is struggling with a particular concept, they can adjust their teaching approach, offer additional resources, or provide one-on-one support. Similarly, real-time data allows students to receive immediate feedback on their performance, helping them identify areas for improvement and adjust their study habits accordingly.

3. Reducing Educational Inequality

AI has the potential to reduce educational inequality by making high-quality education more accessible to underserved populations. Adaptive learning systems can provide personalized instruction to students regardless of their geographic location, socioeconomic background, or learning ability. AI-powered tools can also assist students with disabilities by offering customized support, such as text-to-speech features, closed captions, and alternative learning materials.

By providing equal access to personalized learning experiences, AI can help bridge the gap between privileged and disadvantaged students, contributing to a more equitable education system.

4. AI as a Tool for Lifelong Learning

As the world of work continues to evolve, lifelong learning is becoming increasingly important. AI-powered educational tools make it easier for individuals to engage in continuous learning throughout their lives, whether they are pursuing new skills, changing careers, or seeking personal growth.

Adaptive learning systems can create personalized learning paths for adult learners, helping them acquire new knowledge and skills at their own pace. AI-powered platforms such as Coursera and edX offer a wide range of online courses and certifications, allowing learners to access education from top institutions and industry leaders.

Conclusion

AI and adaptive learning systems are revolutionizing education by providing personalized, data-driven learning experiences that cater to the unique needs of each student. From intelligent tutoring systems to AI-powered LMS platforms, AI is enhancing the learning process by offering tailored support, real-time insights, and scalable solutions. As AI continues to evolve, its impact on education will only deepen, paving the way for a more personalized, accessible, and equitable future in learning.

Chapter 8: The Role of Data Privacy and Ethics in Educational Informatics

---

The integration of advanced technologies into education has fundamentally transformed the way students learn and how institutions operate. Educational informatics—combining data analytics, adaptive learning systems, and artificial intelligence—promises to improve learning outcomes, personalize education, and optimize resource use. However, with the increasing reliance on data-driven systems comes significant concerns about privacy, security, and ethical considerations. As educational institutions collect and process vast amounts of student data, they face the challenge of balancing innovation with the protection of students' rights and privacy.

This chapter delves into the critical issues of data privacy and ethics in educational informatics, discussing concerns surrounding data usage, ethical considerations for handling student information, and how institutions can develop a framework for ethical data use.

Data Privacy Concerns in Educational Technologies

1. The Collection of Student Data

In educational informatics, vast amounts of data are collected from students to personalize learning experiences, track progress, and improve institutional efficiency. This data includes:

- Personal information: Names, dates of birth, contact information, and identification numbers.
- Academic data: Grades, test scores, attendance records, assignments, and participation in online courses.
- Behavioral data: Student interactions with learning management systems (LMS), online activity, learning preferences, and time spent on different tasks.
- Biometric data: In some cases, data such as facial recognition for identity verification, typing patterns, and eye-tracking for engagement analysis.

While this data offers valuable insights for improving education, it also raises significant concerns about privacy, particularly when sensitive information is stored or shared without adequate protection or consent.

2. Risks of Data Breaches

One of the most pressing privacy concerns is the risk of data breaches. Educational institutions and technology platforms are increasingly being targeted by cybercriminals due to the vast amount of sensitive information they hold. If student data is compromised, it can lead to identity theft, fraud, and unauthorized access to personal information.

The vulnerabilities within educational technologies stem from various factors, including outdated security protocols, poor encryption practices, and inadequate staff training on data protection. As more institutions adopt cloud-based storage solutions and third-party services, ensuring the security of student data becomes increasingly complex and requires constant vigilance.

3. Third-Party Data Sharing

Another major concern is the sharing of student data with third-party vendors, such as educational technology providers, data analytics firms, and software developers. Many educational institutions rely on these vendors to provide critical services, including LMS platforms, adaptive learning systems, and assessment tools. However, once student data is shared with third parties, institutions may lose control over how that data is used or protected.

There is also the risk that third-party vendors may use student data for purposes beyond educational enhancement, such as marketing or selling the data to advertisers.

Without strict oversight and transparency, students and their families may be unaware of how their information is being used or misused by external entities.

4. Informed Consent and Student Autonomy

Informed consent is a fundamental principle of data privacy, yet it remains a significant challenge in educational settings. Students, particularly minors, often have little control over the data being collected from them and may not fully understand the implications of sharing their information. Consent forms are frequently bundled with other agreements, making it difficult for students or parents to opt-out of specific data-sharing practices.

Moreover, institutions must balance their legal obligations to protect student privacy with the need to gather data for educational improvement. Finding the right balance between student autonomy and institutional requirements is a complex ethical issue that demands careful consideration.

Ethical Considerations for Student Data

1. The Right to Privacy

Students have a fundamental right to privacy, which must be respected by all educational institutions and technology providers. This right encompasses the ability to control how their personal and academic data is collected, stored, and used. However, as more educational technologies incorporate data analytics and AI, students' privacy rights can be inadvertently compromised.

Ethical data practices in education should prioritize transparency, giving students and their families a clear understanding of what data is being collected and why. Institutions must also ensure that students can exercise control over their own information, including the ability to access, correct, or delete their data.

2. Data Ownership and Control

A key ethical consideration in educational informatics is determining who owns and controls the data collected from students. In most cases, the institution or technology provider retains ownership of the data, even though it is derived from the student's personal and academic activities. This raises concerns about how the data can be used, shared, or sold, especially when the student has little say in the matter.

Institutions must establish clear guidelines regarding data ownership, ensuring that students have a say in how their information is managed. Ethical frameworks should emphasize student empowerment, giving them the ability to consent to data sharing and to revoke that consent at any time.

3. Fairness and Bias in Data Analytics

One of the risks associated with the use of data analytics and AI in education is the potential for bias and unfairness. Algorithms used to analyze student performance, predict academic outcomes, or tailor learning experiences can inadvertently reflect and perpetuate biases, particularly if the data used to train these systems is incomplete or skewed.

For example, AI systems might unintentionally disadvantage certain groups of students based on factors such as socioeconomic status, race, or gender if the algorithms are trained on biased data. This can lead to unequal access to resources, biased grading, or unfair academic evaluations.

Ethical data practices should prioritize fairness, ensuring that AI systems are trained on diverse, representative data sets and that potential biases are identified and mitigated. Institutions must also conduct regular audits of their AI tools to ensure they are not perpetuating inequalities or discrimination.

4. Transparency and Accountability

Transparency is essential for building trust in educational technologies. Students, parents, and educators need to understand how data is being collected, analyzed, and used to inform educational decisions. Institutions must be transparent about the algorithms and models used to personalize learning, assess student performance, or guide instructional strategies.

Additionally, accountability mechanisms should be put in place to ensure that institutions and technology providers are held responsible for the ethical use of student data. This includes the establishment of oversight committees, regular audits, and clear reporting structures to address any misuse of data.

Developing a Framework for Ethical Data Use in Education

To address the ethical challenges associated with data privacy in educational informatics, institutions must develop comprehensive frameworks that outline the principles, policies, and practices for handling student data. An ethical data framework should prioritize privacy, transparency, fairness, and accountability while fostering innovation in education. Here are key components of such a framework:

1. Data Governance Policies

Institutions should implement robust data governance policies that define the collection, storage, and usage of student data. These policies should include:

- Clear guidelines on data collection: What data is collected, how it is used, and how long it is retained.
- Security protocols: Measures to protect data from unauthorized access or breaches, including encryption and access controls.
- Consent processes: Transparent methods for obtaining informed consent from students and parents, with clear opt-out options.

2. Ethical AI and Algorithm Development

As AI and data analytics play a larger role in education, ethical considerations must be built into the development and deployment of these technologies. Institutions should work with AI developers to ensure that algorithms are fair, transparent, and unbiased. Regular audits of AI systems can help identify and correct any biases that may emerge over time.

3. Student Empowerment and Control

An ethical data framework should prioritize student autonomy, giving individuals more control over their data. Institutions can implement tools that allow students to access their information, correct inaccuracies, and manage their data-sharing preferences. Additionally, students should be given clear options to withdraw their consent for data collection at any time.

4. Regular Audits and Reporting

To ensure ongoing accountability, institutions should conduct regular audits of their data practices. These audits should evaluate the effectiveness of data privacy measures, the fairness of AI algorithms, and the overall transparency of data usage. Institutions should also provide regular reports to students and parents, outlining how data is being used to enhance educational outcomes.

Conclusion

The rise of educational informatics offers tremendous opportunities to improve teaching and learning through data-driven insights and personalized approaches. However, these advancements must be accompanied by a strong commitment to data privacy and ethics. By developing comprehensive frameworks that prioritize transparency, fairness, and student empowerment, educational institutions can harness the power of data while protecting the rights and privacy of their students. As technology continues to evolve, maintaining an ethical approach to data use will be essential to fostering trust and ensuring equitable access to quality education for all.

Chapter 9:

Challenges and Opportunities in Learning Informatics

As the digital age continues to reshape nearly every aspect of society, education is no exception. Learning informatics, the intersection of technology, data, and education, holds great potential to revolutionize how we teach, learn, and assess students. By leveraging data-driven systems, personalized learning, and cutting-edge tools, learning informatics promises to enhance student outcomes, optimize teaching strategies, and provide a more customized educational experience. However, the path toward widespread adoption of these technologies is fraught with challenges. At the same time, opportunities for innovation in learning informatics abound, offering a glimpse into a future where data-driven education becomes the norm.

This chapter explores the barriers to adopting educational technologies, the opportunities for innovation in learning informatics, and the potential future of education in a data-driven world.

Barriers to Adoption of Educational Technologies

Despite the transformative potential of learning informatics, several barriers stand in the way of its widespread adoption in educational institutions. These obstacles range from technical limitations to institutional resistance and socio-economic disparities.

1. Lack of Infrastructure and Resources

One of the primary barriers to adopting educational technologies is the lack of infrastructure and resources in many schools and universities. Implementing learning management systems (LMS), personalized learning platforms, and data analytics tools requires reliable internet access, modern hardware, and skilled IT staff to manage these systems. Unfortunately, many institutions, particularly in underserved or rural areas, struggle with limited budgets and inadequate technology infrastructure.

In addition, the costs associated with maintaining and updating these systems can be prohibitive. Schools may face challenges in securing long-term funding to ensure that educational technologies remain functional and up to date. As a result, while some institutions may have access to cutting-edge tools, others may lag behind, leading to unequal opportunities for students.

2. Resistance to Change

Another significant challenge in adopting learning informatics is resistance to change from educators, administrators, and even students. Educational systems are traditionally slow to adapt to new technologies, often due to institutional inertia, fear of the unknown, or skepticism about the effectiveness of digital tools. Teachers and administrators may worry that data-driven systems will replace traditional pedagogical methods or lead to a depersonalization of the learning experience.

Moreover, educators may feel overwhelmed by the steep learning curve associated with using new technologies, particularly if they are not provided with adequate training or support. Some may fear that technology will reduce their control over the classroom, diminishing their role as facilitators of learning. Overcoming this resistance requires effective change management, professional development, and clear communication about the benefits of learning informatics.

3. Data Privacy and Security Concerns

As discussed in the previous chapter, data privacy and security are major concerns in educational informatics. Institutions must carefully manage the sensitive information they collect from students, ensuring compliance with legal frameworks such as the General Data Protection Regulation (GDPR) and the Family Educational Rights and

Privacy Act (FERPA). The risk of data breaches or unauthorized access can make institutions hesitant to adopt data-intensive technologies.

Parents and students may also be wary of how their data is used and whether it could be exploited for purposes beyond education. Addressing these concerns requires robust data governance policies, transparent data practices, and a commitment to ethical data use.

4. Digital Divide

The digital divide—the gap between those with access to technology and those without—represents another significant barrier to the widespread adoption of educational technologies. In many parts of the world, students lack access to reliable internet connections, modern devices, and basic digital literacy skills. This disparity exacerbates existing inequalities in education, leaving some students at a disadvantage in a world that increasingly relies on digital learning tools.

Bridging the digital divide requires targeted efforts from governments, institutions, and technology providers to ensure that all students have equitable access to the resources needed to benefit from learning informatics. Without addressing these socio-economic barriers, the promise of data-driven education will remain out of reach for many.

Opportunities for Innovation in Learning Informatics

While there are challenges to the adoption of learning informatics, there are also significant opportunities for innovation that can transform education. These innovations have the potential to make learning more personalized, efficient, and engaging for both students and educators.

1. Personalized Learning Pathways

One of the most exciting opportunities in learning informatics is the potential to create personalized learning pathways for students. By collecting and analyzing data on student performance, learning preferences, and progress, adaptive learning systems can tailor instruction to meet the unique needs of each learner. This approach moves away from the traditional "one-size-fits-all" model of education, allowing students to learn at their own pace and receive targeted support where needed.

For example, if a student struggles with a particular concept in math, an adaptive learning system can provide additional resources, exercises, or alternative explanations to help them master the material. Conversely, if a student excels in a subject, the system can offer more challenging content to keep them engaged and motivated. Personalized learning has the potential to improve student outcomes by providing a more customized educational experience that caters to individual strengths and weaknesses.

2. Real-Time Data Analytics and Feedback

Another area of innovation in learning informatics is the use of real-time data analytics to provide immediate feedback to students and teachers. In traditional education models, feedback often comes after the fact—through graded assignments, tests, or reports. However, with the power of data analytics, educators can now assess student progress in real time and adjust instruction accordingly.

Real-time feedback allows for more responsive teaching, enabling educators to identify and address learning gaps before they become significant. For students, immediate feedback provides valuable insights into their performance, helping them stay on track and make improvements as they progress through a course. This type of dynamic, data-driven instruction can lead to better learning outcomes and a more engaged student body.

3. Gamification and Engagement

Gamification, the application of game elements in non-game contexts, offers an innovative approach to enhancing student engagement and motivation. Educational games, virtual learning environments, and gamified assessments can make learning more interactive and enjoyable for students. By incorporating elements such as points, levels, badges, and leaderboards, educators can create a sense of competition and achievement that motivates students to stay engaged with the material.

Gamification also encourages active participation and collaboration, particularly in online or remote learning environments. For instance, virtual classrooms can integrate game-based learning activities to promote teamwork, problem-solving, and critical thinking skills. As educational technology continues to evolve, gamification will play an increasingly important role in keeping students motivated and invested in their learning journeys.

4. AI-Powered Teaching Assistants

Artificial intelligence (AI) is playing an increasingly prominent role in education, offering opportunities to automate administrative tasks, enhance personalized learning, and support educators in delivering more effective instruction. AI-powered teaching assistants can help manage routine tasks such as grading, attendance tracking, and answering frequently asked questions, freeing up teachers' time to focus on more complex instructional responsibilities.

In addition, AI can assist in analyzing student data to identify learning patterns, predict academic outcomes, and suggest personalized interventions for struggling students. These AI-driven insights can empower teachers to make more informed decisions about how to support their students' academic growth.

The Future of Education in a Data-Driven World

The future of education will be increasingly shaped by the data-driven insights and technologies that learning informatics brings to the table. As educational institutions continue to embrace these innovations, we can expect several key trends to emerge:

1. Increased Personalization

The future of education will see a greater emphasis on personalized learning, with adaptive technologies providing tailored instruction to meet the needs of individual students. Learning pathways will become more flexible, allowing students to progress at their own pace and receive customized support in real time. This shift toward personalization will likely lead to improved academic outcomes, greater student engagement, and reduced achievement gaps.

2. Blended Learning Models

As virtual classrooms and remote learning tools become more sophisticated, blended learning models—where traditional face-to-face instruction is combined with online learning—will become more prevalent. These models offer the best of both worlds, allowing students to benefit from in-person interactions with teachers and peers while also enjoying the flexibility and convenience of online education.

Blended learning can provide students with greater autonomy over their learning experience, making education more accessible and accommodating to different learning styles and needs.

3. Data-Driven Decision Making

Educational institutions will increasingly rely on data analytics to inform decision-making at every level, from individual classrooms to district-wide policies. By leveraging data-driven insights, administrators and educators can optimize resource allocation, identify trends, and implement interventions that improve student outcomes. As a result, data-driven education will become more efficient, effective, and equitable.

4. Ethical Considerations and Policy Development

As data continues to play a central role in education, there will be a growing need for robust policies and frameworks that address privacy, security, and ethics. Institutions must strike a balance between innovation and the protection of student rights, ensuring that data is used responsibly and transparently. The development of ethical guidelines for the use of AI and data analytics in education will be critical to maintaining trust and accountability in a data-driven educational landscape.

Conclusion

The challenges and opportunities in learning informatics highlight the complexity of integrating technology and data into education. While barriers such as infrastructure limitations, resistance to change, and privacy concerns present significant hurdles, the potential for personalized learning, real-time feedback, and AI-powered innovations offer exciting possibilities for the future of education. As institutions navigate these challenges, the thoughtful application of learning informatics has the power to transform how we teach, learn, and assess in the 21st century. The key to success will lie in embracing innovation while remaining mindful of the ethical and practical implications of data-driven education.

Chapter 10: Conclusion

The Long-Term Impact of Informatics on Education

As the world becomes increasingly interconnected through digital technologies, the role of informatics in education will continue to expand and evolve. Learning informatics, driven by the integration of data analytics, artificial intelligence, and personalized learning systems, has already begun to transform the educational landscape. This transformation is expected to have long-term implications, reshaping the way students learn, educators teach, and institutions operate.

1. Personalized Learning at Scale

One of the most significant long-term impacts of informatics on education will be the widespread adoption of personalized learning. Informatics allows for the continuous collection and analysis of data on student progress, learning preferences, and behaviors. This data-driven approach makes it possible to tailor educational experiences to the unique needs of individual learners on a large scale.

As adaptive learning systems become more advanced, students will receive personalized learning pathways, customized feedback, and real-time support. This level of personalization will foster greater engagement, improve academic outcomes, and empower learners to take ownership of their education. Over time, this shift will lead to more equitable and inclusive learning environments, where students of all abilities and backgrounds can thrive.

2. Data-Driven Decision Making in Education

Informatics will also play a pivotal role in shaping how educational institutions make decisions. With the ability to collect vast amounts of data, schools and universities will be able to assess their teaching methods, curriculum effectiveness, and student performance more accurately than ever before. Data-driven decision-making will enable educators and administrators to identify areas for improvement, allocate resources more efficiently, and develop strategies that enhance the overall learning experience.

Furthermore, educational institutions will be able to use predictive analytics to forecast student success and intervene early when students are at risk of falling behind. By leveraging data insights, schools will be better equipped to provide targeted support to both struggling and high-achieving students, ultimately leading to more successful learning outcomes.

3. Transforming the Role of Educators

The role of educators is also expected to change in response to advances in learning informatics. Rather than focusing solely on content delivery, teachers will increasingly take on the role of facilitators and guides. With AI-powered tools and data analytics handling routine tasks such as grading, lesson planning, and tracking student progress, educators will have more time to focus on personalized instruction, mentoring, and providing emotional and social support to students.

Teachers will become data-literate professionals, equipped with the skills to interpret student data and use it to inform their teaching strategies. This shift will require ongoing professional development and training to ensure that educators are prepared to leverage technology effectively. Over time, the integration of informatics will enhance the teaching profession, enabling educators to deliver more impactful and meaningful learning experiences.

How to Prepare for Future Changes in Educational Technologies

As educational technologies and informatics continue to evolve, it is crucial for students, educators, and institutions to prepare for the changes ahead. By proactively embracing innovation and developing strategies for integrating new technologies, educational stakeholders can stay ahead of the curve and ensure that they are well-positioned to navigate the future of learning.

1. Embrace Lifelong Learning and Digital Literacy

In a rapidly changing digital world, students and educators alike must prioritize lifelong learning. As new technologies emerge, it is essential to continuously develop digital literacy skills, staying up to date with the latest tools and trends in educational technology. Schools and universities should foster a culture of innovation, encouraging both students and staff to experiment with new technologies and approaches to learning.

By cultivating a mindset of adaptability and openness to change, educational institutions can better prepare for the inevitable shifts in the educational landscape. Lifelong learning will become a cornerstone of success, enabling individuals to thrive in a dynamic and technology-driven world.

2. Invest in Infrastructure and Professional Development

To fully realize the potential of learning informatics, educational institutions must invest in the necessary infrastructure and professional development programs. This includes upgrading technological resources, ensuring access to reliable internet connectivity, and providing educators with the training they need to use digital tools effectively. Schools and universities should prioritize the creation of robust IT support systems that can manage the complexities of learning informatics platforms.

Additionally, ongoing professional development for teachers is critical. Educators must be equipped with the skills to interpret data, use AI-powered tools, and deliver personalized instruction. Investing in teacher training and development will not only improve the quality of education but also empower teachers to play an active role in shaping the future of learning.

3. Adopt Ethical Data Practices

As data becomes an increasingly central component of education, institutions must prioritize ethical data practices to protect student privacy and build trust. Developing comprehensive data governance policies, implementing secure data storage solutions, and ensuring compliance with legal regulations such as GDPR and FERPA are essential steps in safeguarding student information.

Educational institutions should also promote transparency in how data is collected, analyzed, and used. Clear communication with students, parents, and educators about the benefits and risks of data-driven education will help build trust and ensure that informatics is used responsibly. By adopting ethical data practices, schools and universities can create a safe and secure environment for learning.

Final Thoughts on the Role of Informatics in Shaping the Future of Learning

Learning informatics represents a powerful force for change in education, offering unprecedented opportunities to improve the quality of learning and teaching. From personalized learning systems to data-driven assessments, informatics has the potential to revolutionize education, making it more efficient, inclusive, and effective. However, the successful integration of informatics will require careful planning, investment, and a commitment to ethical data use.

As we look to the future, it is clear that the role of technology and data in education will only continue to grow. Educational institutions, educators, and students must remain agile and adaptable, embracing innovation while staying mindful of the ethical implications of data-driven learning. The future of education lies at the intersection of technology and human creativity, and learning informatics will play a central role in shaping this new era of learning.

By harnessing the power of informatics, we have the opportunity to create a more personalized, equitable, and data-informed educational system that empowers learners and educators alike. The journey toward this future will be challenging, but the potential rewards are immense. As we move forward, it is up to all of us to embrace the possibilities of learning informatics and work together to shape a brighter future for education.

Author's Note

As we stand on the cusp of a digital revolution in education, the integration of informatics into learning offers exciting possibilities. My journey in writing this book, Education and Learning Informatics: Transforming the Future of Education with Data and Technology, has been shaped by a passion for understanding how data and technology are transforming education. The concepts of personalized learning, adaptive technologies, data analytics, and AI in education have opened new horizons for educators, students, and institutions alike.

I firmly believe that the power of learning informatics will redefine the role of teachers and learners, creating a more equitable, efficient, and personalized learning experience for all. While the possibilities are inspiring, it is crucial to recognize the challenges and ethical considerations that come with the use of data in education. Protecting student privacy and fostering transparency must remain top priorities as we continue to innovate.

Through this book, I hope to provide insight into the transformative potential of learning informatics and spark thoughtful discussion about its role in shaping the future of education. My goal is to inspire educators, administrators, and learners to embrace these tools while remaining mindful of their ethical implications. Thank you for taking this journey with me, and I encourage you to stay curious, adaptable, and open to the exciting future that awaits us in the world of learning informatics.

— Oluchi Ike

References

1. Siemens, G., & Baker, R. (2012). Learning analytics and educational data mining: Towards communication and collaboration. In Proceedings of the 2nd International Conference on Learning Analytics and Knowledge.

2. Johnson, L., Adams Becker, S., Estrada, V., & Freeman, A. (2015). NMC Horizon Report: 2015 Higher Education Edition. Austin, Texas: The New Media Consortium.

3. Pardo, A., & Siemens, G. (2014). Ethical considerations and learning analytics. In Journal of Learning Analytics, 1(1), 120-127.

4. Luckin, R., Holmes, W., Griffiths, M., & Forcier, L. B. (2016). Intelligence unleashed: An argument for AI in education. Pearson Education.

5. Ullmann, T. D. (2019). Data-driven education: A key research area for learning analytics and the impact of artificial intelligence. Springer.

6. Picciano, A. G. (2012). The evolution of big data and learning analytics in American higher education. In Journal of Asynchronous Learning Networks, 16(3), 9-20.

7. Kay, R. H., & LeSage, A. (2009). Examining the benefits and challenges of using audience response systems: A review of the literature. In Computers & Education, 53(3), 819-827.

8. Knox, J. (2017). Data power in education: Exploring critical awareness with the "Learning Analytics Report Card." In Teaching in Higher Education, 22(4), 1-16.

9. Williamson, B. (2017). Big data in education: The digital future of learning, policy, and practice. SAGE Publications.

10. West, D. M. (2012). Big data for education: Data mining, machine learning, and information retrieval in education. Government Studies at Brookings.

Further Resources

➤ Learning Analytics and Knowledge Conference (LAK): A premier event focused on the latest research and applications in learning analytics. lakconference.org

➤ EDUCAUSE: A nonprofit association that supports the advancement of higher education through the intelligent use of information technology. [educause.edu](https://www.educause.edu/)

➤ International Society for Technology in Education (ISTE): A community of global educators who believe in the power of technology to transform learning. [iste.org](https://www.iste.org/)

➢ Future of Education Technology Conference (FETC): A leading event for exploring the latest innovations in educational technology. [fetc.org](https://www.fetc.org/)

➢ The Journal of Educational Data Mining (JEDM): A leading source for research on how data mining methods apply to education. [educationaldatamining.org](http://www.educationaldatamining.org/)

➢ Pearson's AI and Learning Resources: Information and reports on AI-driven educational technologies. [pearson.com](https://www.pearson.com)

➢ The Open University's FutureLearn Program: Courses on learning analytics and data-driven education. [futurelearn.com](https://www.futurelearn.com)

These resources will help you explore the fast-evolving landscape of learning informatics and stay updated on new developments in educational technologies.